Laid Bare

Avery Grace

BookLeaf Publishing

India | USA | UK

Laid Bare © 2022 Avery Grace

All rights reserved.

Presentation by *BookLeaf Publishing*

Web: www.bookleafpub.com

E-mail: info@bookleafpub.com

ISBN: 9789357446495

First edition 2022

DEDICATION

To Trea, Xavier, Darla, and Tuna, for being my deepest teachers. And to the other teachers/readers alive and passed, who along the way have cheerleader-ed my writing from its infancy, through its adolescence, and hopefully now to some on-going state of maturity.

As my zen teacher would say, "hands together," or I bow to you. On these hands are tattooed "Don't" on one, and "Know" on the other--the phrase which can only be seen in *gassho*. I could never have known that all of your support would culminate into this offering, and more.

I offer my fear

upon the altar

of your revealing

your True Self.

May any obstacle

from me to you

be shattered

into a thousand

glittering pieces

with which to paint

the night.

This way,

when lovers look up

they see

what is possible

when each is willing

to face themselves

and become a well

for the other.

Avery Grace, 2021.

ACKNOWLEDGEMENT

To Khāwje Shams-od-Dīn Moḥammad Ḥāfeẓ-e Shīrāzī, or simply Hafiz, whose poetry sustains me everyday. And for Rābiʿa, an earlier female Sufi ancestor, for her inspiring me to love all that I fear. And for Kiran and Jeanne, the hands that connect me to them in this life through community and family.

For Mark Manson, encouraging me--albeit electronically--to find and cultivate the things that, "make [me] forget to shit". And the dirty minimalists--interviews with Gordon Lish whose uncompromising editorial eye I find applicable to all writing, and to Chuck Palahniuk in particular, who surrendered the fact that if I was dedicated to becoming an author, nothing he could say would stop me.

And that if I wasn't, there would be nothing he could say that would make me one.

To Audre Lorde and other poets of color, known and unknown, for your contribution to a more just and anti-colonial world, and your truths helping me engage into anti-racist, anti-settler colonial capitalism in smallways each day.

PREFACE

Occasionally I'm asked, "why do you write?"
My answer is always the same, even after you
sift through the top layers: "oh, to process
things," or, "I've had a colorful lifethat folx don't
know about". And, "I've got a punchy way of
writing that others find interesting".

Now be this self-centered as it may, underneath
all that strata of response to the most spiritual
and non-spiritual question this is-"why?"--is
t=home to the true answer:

I write because I can't not write.

I write because writing demands that I write.
Even if no one else ever reads it. Writing, the
Muse, she won't leave me be unless I attend to
her. The Muse and the Craft only take prisoners.
Grateful, ecstatic prisoners for whom working to
the bone leaves only the pulsating, naked heart.

I offer this heart as sacrifice upon the altar of
authentic being.

If my entire day went to shit and I literally made
every possible mistake that day, was totally

unproductive in all other ways and missed a
once in a lifetime opportunity, f I wrote, it was a
good day.

Success resides in the process. =If I can hold
that lens against the colonial and capitalistic
demand for production and commodification, for
outcome, thenI have a shot at being successful
(and happy) everyday.

With writing. With everything.

A Petition and Offering to My Ancestors

Ancestors,
spirits of blood
and bone,lace
and work,
I call to you and offer
my effort, my attention,
my love in this life, so
you may know
regard and well-being
in this life
and the next.

Liquor and smoke,
sugar and snacks,
may you know ease
and pleasure
in ways you
may not
ave while alive.

I honor your suffering,
your struggle,
I continue to come
to know you, asking

that you speak
for yourself.

You are remembered.

That which is remembered
 lives.
May my gaze, my listening, my
Visits,
keep you company.
Be a bridge
for your work
and desires
here.

I ask only for
your presence,
your guidance,
so that I may do my best
work in this life.

I ask to be in right relationship with you,
One born of and sustained by
respect, connection, levity, and power.

May our work together
nourish us both, may I
be your vessel for change
In this world.

As above.
So below.

So mote it be.

Culling Ghosts

The day I cut my mother
From of my life, I
culled myself
of former generations
of pain, and spared
the young ones
in my care.

I will not be a host, a
willing channel,
for the flow of
dis-ease,
a plague of my
and many
lineages. Too many
pollutants, invisible
toxins,
to try and purify
by one being
in one lifetime.

So, I looked
into my mother's eyes
for the last time,
and cut my heart

and held the children
within—so those without,might know freedom.

Freedom, from
any ghosts
that would otherwise
come
through me.

When they sleep now,
my, our, children,
they need not fear
for I will not be the specter
that children fear in the night
or worse—by day;

I will be the night,
the light that soothes,
the hearth fire that warms,
a cool well
to which
they can return.

An imperfect guardian
of unconditional love.

But don't be fooled
by my sentimental gushing—
I, am still learning

how. Will always be learning
how—to be, to offer
that which I was never
shown, the gifts I was never
given. The rock upon which
I was never
offered
to rest.

And so, I sit
As a rock, as a mountain
your willing pupil,
Little Ones,
My ruest teachers.

Our soft fulcrum
by which the young
always teach the old.

Suffering

The two-year-old
crashes
against the rocks
of reality,
the tide of his wants a
vicious
relentless
flow.

Stumbling,
drunk on expectation,
he rages.
Not knowing yet,
he is simply raging
at life.

In my snide
Loving-Kindness,
I quip,
"Today we repeat
our lesson of the First
Noble Truth
of Suffering."

Not allowed
by his overlords
to ride his tricycle

naked in the snow,
he puddles,
sobbing face down
into the bosom
of the earth.

Pachamama receives him.
Resentful tears
 stain her skin.

I again
let him in
on our most human secret:

"It doesn't get much
ifferent than this,
my friend.
It pretty much stays
the same
from here on out.
Welcome".

This may seem perhaps

only mildly helpful.
But it is the fiercest truth
I know.

As I watch

the tragic miracle
of the growth of an ego—
"Mine! More!"
the epitomical "No!"—
I think to ways
in which I, we,
are exactly the same.

The nights I
screech at god—
my own tantrums,
swaddled and witnessed,
every human problem,
every flavor of pain,
coming down to thinking:

It is, I am, you are—
mine.

Or the grave spiritual offense
of assuming:

That this is, you are, I am—
not enough.

Or if one prefers,
the Cliff Notes
of adult, childish arrogance—
meet the circumstances of your life,

meet the truth,
with a "no".

Meanwhile,
the puddle collects
Chimself the violence
of his demands
ebbing and recessing
temporarily.

Just like yours.

Blood Circle

In your
feral grief
wild, you gnaw
off your own
and the limbs
of others.

Small limbs.
Childs' limbs.
Small hearts.
Your own blood.

Casualties
of your suffering.
Of your unexamined
history,
of your untamed
reactivity.

Blinded by rage,
wounds—old
 and new—and
unacknowledged
expectation, your

self righteousness, your
victimhood forms

a blood circle.

Anything in reach
of the blade
of your painriskslaceration.

But in reliving the past
in the present
you cannot see
crimson footprints
haunting your steps.

Cannot see that
unwillingness to look
heralds your possession.

I watch as
Hafiz's Mirror does:
reflecting,
abiding,
loving.

And I pray.
I pray for
your wakefulness,
lest the burden of
wreckageeft
in your wake

be too much
for you to bear.

Or lest the truths
of these moments
also go unseen
unacknowledged.
Their wisdom
squandered.
Allowing the cycle of
pain to continue

in the three-limbed
and wounded-hearted.

Greatest Teacher

I understand now
why those wiser
than I have said,

"The one who causes you the
most distress is
your greatest teacher".

I resisted, at first.
New-age, hippy
bullshit.
Pollyanna.

Fuck you, Pema (1).
You didn't even
raise your own children—
true story.

As I sitearing
witness, feeling
the intensity of
conflict
inside this body,
I am in awe
of what it means

to be alive.

But still,
to the Divine
I retort:

"You're fucking welcome."and,
"Are you entertained?"

But once I've exhausted
my smallness,
my ordinary
human complaints:

"*Thank you.*"

Struck still and
wordless,
now I hold
this breath with
thoughtless appreciation—
for the depth of love,
pain, and grief,
that is possible.
boundless,
and yet contained
within the bounds
of this body.

(1)- Reference to Pema Chodron, a famous
Western Buddhist teacher and author of popular
spiritual and self-help books, most notably,
"When Things Fall Apart".

Spoiled milk

We
are the Sacrifice.

We
re the Sacrifice
Generation.

Those without
true elders.
Those who have had
to become
elders, stewards,
guardians,
and parents.
Our own
parents.

Never before have
children been asked
to rise,
asked to raise
siblings, parents,
descendants, communities—
simultaneously. And,
alone.

We are those.

We are those
asked to guide
our descendants,
our wayward
would-be elders—
future ancestors—
into our
dystopian
inheritance.

You say you do not
understand us--that
if only we worked hard
Enough, the table
scrapes would be ours
For the taking

But you,
past generations, who
in your short-sighted
growth-obsessed
narcissism,
left
us.

Left us and
left our children,
left your grandchildren,
an ecological and

colonial debt that
Humanity
may never be able to repay.

You cannot know
the rage of
generations fed
unrequited promises,
straight
from your teat.

Generations ago,
somewhere you learned that
all you had to do
was feed us—
feed our mouths but not
our souls.
Feed yourselves but not
the Earth.

All you've offered is
spoiled milk.
Ofchildhood,
and adulthood.

There is a reason that
Indigenous, First
Nations people speak
of Seven Generations.

You exterminated
this wisdom.
And there is no
statue of limitations
on this crime.

Yet, like children
you take everything
but responsibility
for your own
steps.

How can children have
such heavy footprints
and leave
such a deep
depression?

Children are taught
to walk with awareness.
We have taught ourselves.
And we have had to
teach you,
spitting and crying,
kicking and screaming
in your
denial.

If some part of you can
finally feel
reverence,
You may call us
The Pivot.

We are the Pivot.
The Pivot in
behavior, in
healing, in
atonement, in
cosmology.

We are where
that which must stop, stops.
And where the new
begins.

Atonement

My dear,
I'm sorry.

Again
I've held you responsible.

It wasn't you
who held me to the floor.

It wasn't.
And yet—

I ask that you atone.

That you walk
a tightrope over eggshells,

Live an eternal apology
for another's crime.

It's unfair.
It's unrealistic.

And yet—the little people
inside me scream

for blood.

Someone's blood.
Anyone's blood.

After all—

their veins were opened,
their childhood--
Joy
Ease
Trust—

Leeched.
Drained.

For others.

Now my little children
must be fed,

Satiated,

Before their cries can transform
into they authentic notes
in this grand symphony.

A Letter to My Grandfather

I touch myself
in places that were once blank.

What was before
a No Man's Land—
restricted, absent,
even to me—
has through great labor
and pain
bursted with harvest.

A harvest of
restoration, of
reclamation, of
reception and
revolution.

My fingers dance
in the warm earth of my pelvis
coming to know the land.
The gate of my mind opens,

I venture into fantasy,
the horizon less obstructed.

And with every caress
I anoint myself
with freedom
from the past.

In this way,
every fuck becomes a sacrament.
Every orgasm an act of resistance.

Every moment of trust
an act of resilience.
Every moment of savoring,
salvation.

Every moan making up
for every muffled cry
and unspoken truth
from that hotel room
at ten years old.

And what that boy has to say is:

This is my body
This is my sex
This is my pleasure!

And I am here.

I am here to claim
my ordinary
divine
birthright.

Healing culled,
an earthen alchemy.
My fields are no longer fallow.
I am reclaiming
pleasure and possibility
from a lifetime
of forced famine.

No Due Process
(in Polyamory)

Each time you walk
out the door
I see my mama's back.

Each time you get ready
for a date,
I see you getting ready

to forget me.

Mama.

You who were supposed
to protect me.
Supposed to know

What he'd do.

What he did.

But you're not my mother.

Today you get ready
to live the agreement
we negotiated,
the agreement we
consented to.

But even with all our principles

your perfect strokes
of eyeliner
are a sharpie
through my name.

They say I'm a write off,
a shed commitment.
penciled in
at best.

You put on that dapper jacket
you never wear
at home—evidence
that there's something
special
about this time.

About this one.

Something good, which means
something dangerous.

Or so the heat
rising from my gut
demanding my attention, insists.

You see,
you might like them.

Which would be
like a coffin nail.
My inner child cries--

Bad things happen
when you leave
me. I say this
to my mother
in your body.

Bad things.

We have a commitment,
a history
of truthfulness—

Yet my hurt still
deems it sentencing without
due process.

Past evidence, exhibit A:

for which you had
a solid alibi.

But you come home.
And you
love me no less.

Teaching that child
that none of it
was true.

That trust is possible.

Raw

Each day we choose
that which
keeps us down.
Caging
our own potential.

Each of us
a chimp
behind bars
lamenting
the treatment
y the captors
e've established.

Masturbating ourselves
with the our lock's key.

Self pity, victimhood—
Small Self porn.

We look out
from our self-
incarceration,
feral.
Ready to spear
any constrictions with
our blame.

Looking for a patsy
to pin on,
the crimes we commit
against ourselves.

Crimes against
our
throbbing,
volcanic,
Authenticity.

But when you feel
yourself
rubbing yourself
raw,
remember,
you chose this.

Regardless of what's happened,
what if you chose this?

Even this?
Even that.

Ownership,
awareness,
your own
internal salve.

Slide into ease,
lube your life with
the balm of empowerment
that only you can produce.

Burn

Allah, yahweh,
Jehovah, shàngdì,
our Father, Earth Mother
God, *dios,*—
it is you,
Rābiʿa, who
teaches us to love
not fear
god or
whatever name,
pronoun,
we rever.

They are all
delightful, child-like
offerings we give
it, her, him, them.

As a child,
as a child,
trying to name
trying to make
sense
of this magic.

How could I
in one moment judge,

despise, "hallowbe thy name,"
with, "*In-sha-allah*,"
on my lips,
the next?

Instead I claim,
whomever you are,
hallow be thy name and
God willing,
inshallah--
for like you,
Rābi 'a,
I want to run
through the streets
with water and flame
extinguishing
the fires of hell and burning
down the promises
of Paradise and
instead
burn

in the extinguishing
of my delusions
of separation,
so I may
simply
love.

Altar

"Hi sexy I do love trans, it's one of my fetishes."

"I just want to have fun,
Baby.
I'd like to play with you,
would love to see your cock,
Baby".

"I'm very curious, you're trans, correct?
Are you able to enjoy receptive intercourse?
One of my fetishes is feminine swallowing.
Any interest? ::wink wink::"

What they
don't tell you
when you're trans—
well,
trans feminine
that is—

is that
you become
an unconsenting
repository:

A barf bag.
A urinal cake.
A diaper—
of fetish,
kink and
secrets.

An object.

"Mouth open always, Mistress.
I would love for you to make me
Cross dress and service your gorgeous
Girl cock, like a slut.

After spanking me soundly, of course.
A ball gag would only get in the way
And deprive you of my cries and moans."

Another name
for where you place
that which you hide,
that which you cherish,
and fear, is
an altar.

I am an altar.

For your buried shame,
your unspoken fantasy.
That which you
do not speak
to your wife,
your children,
your family.

Your priest.

A flesh and blood
confessional booth, I am
custodian,
guardian,
priestess
of liberation.

Your liberation.
From the colonial
oppression of
your desires.

Liberation through
being oppressed.
A tits and dick
Bodhisattva,
revered—

whilst used

A Sex Worker Prayer

I close these
everwatching eyes
afraid, relieved,
to be inside.

Molasses
breathing in,
touching, caressing
the tight space
the hurt space.

The upper residence of
the tremble that
lives in these hips—
dispatches
from a hurt child
and a hurt sex,
from long ago.

I reintroduce
myself to myself,
bridging this
Self
with this Self.

Claiming all of me.

And from this,
the words on my lips
and on my soul are:

May I be all of me so
I can be
with all of you.
All of you, each
of you, as you come.
As you cum.
As you come to cum,
or cum to come,
to grace and truth.

To yourself,
your Self.
Our Self.

And as you cum, come,
into greater clarity,
as the image of your
True Worth
focuses, a
divine aperture
widening,
your view
elongating.

For just that moment,
hopefully, with time,
you savor the taste
of the divine within you.

Your pleasure birthright.

Until that time,
know that I see you.
I see your divinity
bulging
through your skin,
running down your legs,
aching to be felt
and demanding
to be known.

As you come back
from your sojourn
reminded of the truth,
eyes rolling back
to the front of your head,
yours and mine meet.
It is our final touching,
this time.

A touch of knowing
through gaze.

Like Paper

I kneel, prostrated
between your lower limbs
forehead to the back
of your hands
reveling
in the Quiet Gift
of being with you.

One day this skin
will be like paper.

This skin
your hands—
parchment,
upon which you've
written your life.

Like paper.
Life paper.

Dorsum
scars and burns—
administered by the weather
of your life.
Scoring one side,

each a story
of change.

Other marks
palmar, cultivated
with intention.
Knicks
from the building,
the building
of your life.

You have held both
life and death
in these hands.
Who, who
will have the honor
of holding them
at your death?

At that moment
of you exhaling the
final whisper of divinity
that you have to offer,
may the felt sense be the same
as the day
I prostrated before you—

a contentment,
pregnant and ordinary.

Burning is a Gift

Your greatest gift?
When you yell

in my face,
"Where's your fire?!"

You mean the fire
that melts shadow, that ignites

the spark of anger, of
transformation.

But then again, perhaps this gift
is greater:

the respectful allowance,
the requirement,

that I light my own way.

So I remain
a torch.

And you see, torches,
they can burn.

But it's this pain

we've come to heal.

And so,
I burn.

Sometimes torches cauterize;
sometimes they burn houses down.

Houses we hide in. Structures
we no longer need.

Two Rings

There were two rings
in the desert
but there were no bells
nearby.
The humble Junipers,
majestic
as they watched
two people cry.

Together they cried,
together, about and for
things that were not
new, yet, somehow
were—pristine and
with rough edges.

You see they each
carried rocks.
Rocks to be
Tumbled,
of course.

Didn't you hear?

That tumbling, that
polishing—
these are
the purposes
of Union.

The Day the Maple
Leaves Were Silent

"Every leaf and every tree
is a Divine messenger
from a realm unseen
the leaf and the tree
sing a wordless song
you, my friend
listen with an inner ear.
It's a blessing."
-Rumi

Today might be the day
It ends.

Today might be the day
"We" end.

It's a Friday, though
in quarantine who could know?

The maple leaves,
Usually dancing playfully

with the afternoon wind, are
unusually still.

Effulgent chartreuse,
the late afternoon sun
exposing their insides, their veins—
exposing the intimate relationship
we have with them—
they can't hide
anything.

It's a time I call
"God Time," when
the veil always seems thin
and even—I risk to say
in these times—
optimistic.

Usually the leaves,
aside from dancing,
also quiver,
as if Spirit whispers,
"It's alright".

Even though it's not.

But today, the leaves
of the grand maples
are still.

Silent.

Though the same light shows
through, it's a
noticeable departure,
especially given the
tension that preceded it.

"There's nothing you can do
To make this love go away".

Our declaration, among other
in-the-moment truths
we shared
in our beginning.

But like most new lovers, we
proclaimed without much
evidence, beyond our truest aspirations,
A bit drunk
on our own dopamine
and oxytocin, the
fermented fruits
of our co-conspiring
cerebral pharmacies.

Now, who knows.

All one can do, is sit.

Continue to listen
and watch
the divine game play
itself out. To listen
with an inner ear
to the silent maples.

Perhaps this today,
what it seeks to experience is
Loss and grief.

And of so,
it's a blessing.

And I surrender.

Babygirl

I really only come
super hard
when I'm your daughter.

Or your student.
Or that kid you babysit.

I'm never Daddy,
never Mommy,
never Teacher
nor Officer,
not Master
nor Mistress.

I am
Babygirl.

An aside:
it's not about
domme-ing or subbing.
Not about
top or bottom.

It's about what gets me lost.

It's about what takes me back.

In kink we dance
with our darkness
Acknowledged or not.

In the words of Reverend Cash:
"What's done in the dark
will be brought to the light".

That which is shunned
unspoken,
in most circles,
seeks emergence into
the Light, into
the known.

The gravitational pull of
what needs healing,
tugging ever towards the
Core, from which we
dust off traumas,
where we
transmute suffering.

They live in your fantasies,
you know—our wounds.
Gifts, if handled with care.

Babygirl.
I'm always the Little Girl
because the Little Boy
had to flee
Inwards.
Hiding.
Shhh...

You're always Daddy
because Mommy feels
too dangerous.
Too familiar—
even if it wasn't her.

Incest. Abuse. Ironically
aren't sexy
topics, not even
amongst the average
kinkster—even hard players
have their safe words.
Their limits on what's
too painful to hear.
To know.
To experience.

But it is things as they are.
It is my truth.
My survival story, nay, my
Opus of Resilience.

And it plays out
In
Every
Way
I
Want
to
Play.

Sex is sacred.
But some of ours is
is haunted
by hungry ghosts
of the past.
Parasites of spirit.
Ancestors not having
done their work,

leaving it to us.

By the way, it's not, "cum".
C-U-M,
It's "come,"
C-O-M-E.
I don't care what
the Urban Dictionary says.

It's come, as in

come to awareness, as in
come to self, as in
come to grace.

Sex may be transcendent
but transcending isn't
always an upward motion,
but an inward
journeying.

So, we spiral.
Into the center,
Riding the line
going to the heart,
facing what's there.
And what's there
Is hurt.

A hurt that goes unknown
continues to hurt. Self.
And others.

So watch yourself
with inside eyes.

I do, as I play.
As I feel the drag
of being small, of
being objectified, of

being Used.

At times I've felt
like a junkie to a needle.

But that pull--
it can be
a meditation bell.

It can be a call
to awakeness, a call
to speaking—exteriorly,
and interiorly, to those
hiding children.

God Time

Nothing quite as pristine
as a nap and tea
in secret—

afternoons,
when others have forgotten
the day's private gift,
the lost sacred teaching
of Siesta.

The last of the sun's full brilliance
leaking through leaves,
or blinds. Blinding,
but delightfully so.
I am bathed,
caressed, teased,
with warmth.

God time.

Monasteries the world over
swear by the offerings
of pre-dawn for
its closeness
to the Divine.

Clearly they've
yet to hear of this. The call, the resplendent
Soundless Voice
of late afternoon, making
priests, monks, shamans, sheiks,
resemble
used car salesmen.

I implore you—
stare into the sky
before our Friend takes its leave,
exiting stage left, the
Next Act approaching.

And as I lay, both
heavy and light,
living the moment's perfection,
I think that
even if the best of friend
from far away
whom I hadn't seen in years
were slated to arrive,
part of me would silently scream
in my still ecstasy,

Please don't come.

I Don't Space You Because I Care

I know you'd like to remain
distracted.
Ignorant.
But before you get upset
that I
accused you of
the I-word,
take a breath.

Because I care I'm not going to spare you—
rising sea levels in Bangladesh
are the least of your worries.

No water in Phoenix,
Drought in Iowa.
Tampa, slammed
repeatedly,
every
year.

Hurricanes—
they'll have to be numerated—
you'll run out of letters.

And besides,
whoever heard of one that started
with X?

In the Pacific they're called typhoons.
They're worse there too.
No escape,
even in paradise.

Designer respirators,
they're all the rage now—
California, Oregon.
You'd like to lament
your burning lungs,
But you can't spare
the breath I asked
you to take
Earlier.

Nevertheless, try
breathing
again.

Know that
you have joined
the rest of the world
in our climatic
suffering.

It was easier to ignore
when the laments were in Chinese.
Or Hindi—
wasn't it?

Our responsibility,
our inheritance.
Human greed,
"Need,"
short sighted
and the logical conclusion
to a system and ideology
that assumes
and demands
infinite growth.

Meanwhile,
at the Equator,
it will be too hot
to sweat.

Let me say that again:
it will be too hot
to sweat.

Illegal immigration
won't be
caravans of hope
from Central America.

It'll be you, me,
clamoring
to be:
Canadian.
Icelandic.
God forbid,
even Russian.

Can you define peak oil?
It's code.
Code for
not enough
to bring food to your city.

Do you know how to farm?
How to heal
with our herbal allies
who live amongst you?
If there are any left.

I'm sorry
it's come to this, but
ripping off the
blinders of denial
is painful work.

But I do this,
Because I care.

It sounds similar,
but it's different from,
"it's for your own good."

Hate me if you'd like but remember,
your indignation's true name is
Shared Culpability.

Mandate

I awoke
and for seemingly no reason,
it was clear:

This body is still alive
because it has something to offer
today.

This Truth arose from within,
a reminder
of the once-known wisdom
in every child:

Enter your day
like you once entered this life—
with a clear mandate.

We are each a vessel—
a particular tone of
vibrancy in Life's palette.
A symphonic note, an exotic flavor—

but what turned the curry bland,
what robbed the bizcochito
of its sweetness?

This body is pregnant.
With consciousness,
but also with the pain,
loss, and misunderstanding—
of a cadre of ancestors.

They say that patterns continue
until someone in the line
is willing to feel them.

I am willing to feel.

I accept my mandate of
embodying alchemy, of
transmuting shame, of
bearing its child—

the tissues of my body hang
like soaked clothing
following the storm
that has raged
across generations.

Others sought refuge without,
rather than within.

But you cannot do the work
of the crucible

without facing the fire.

So I will feel.

So our ancestors,
our children,
of body and of spirit,
may readily know
their original
pristine and
placid Heart.